BUILDING BY DESIGN

ENGINEERING
THE PYRAMIDS
OF GIZA

BY CHRISTINE ZUCHORA-WALSKE

CONTENT CONSULTANT
Michel Barsoum
Distinguished Professor, Materials Science and Engineering
Drexel University

Cover image: Giza's pyramids are among the world's
oldest, largest, and most impressive landmarks.

Core Library

An Imprint of Abdo Publishing
abdopublishing.com

abdopublishing.com

Published by Abdo Publishing, a division of ABDO, PO Box 398166,
Minneapolis, Minnesota 55439. Copyright © 2018 by Abdo Consulting
Group, Inc. International copyrights reserved in all countries. No part of this
book may be reproduced in any form without written permission from the
publisher. Core Library™ is a trademark and logo of Abdo Publishing.

Printed in the United States of America, North Mankato, Minnesota
092017
012018

THIS BOOK CONTAINS
RECYCLED MATERIALS

Cover Photo: Dan Breckwoldt/Shutterstock Images
Interior Photos: Dan Breckwoldt/Shutterstock Images, 1; Dorling Kindersley/Getty Images, 4–5;
Shutterstock Images, 7, 43; Orhan Cam/Shutterstock Images, 9; Anneke Swanepoel/Shutterstock
Images, 12–13; Felix Bonfils/Library of Congress/Corbis Historical/Getty Images, 16–17; Gary
Hincks/Science Source, 18; Marcello Bertinetti/Science Source, 21; Henning Dalhoff/Science
Source, 24–25, 45; Robert Brook/Science Source, 27; Claus Lunau/Science Source, 29; José Antonio
Peñas/Science Source, 32; De Agostini Picture Library/Getty Images, 34; iStockphoto, 36–37; Ed
Giles/Getty Images News/Getty Images, 40

Editor: Arnold Ringstad
Imprint Designer: Maggie Villaume
Series Design Direction: Laura Polzin

Publisher's Cataloging-in-Publication Data

Names: Zuchora-Walske, Christine, author.
Title: Engineering the Pyramids of Giza / by Christine Zuchora-Walske.
Description: Minneapolis, Minnesota : Abdo Publishing, 2018. | Series: Building by design |
        Includes online resources and index.
Identifiers: LCCN 2017946940 | ISBN 9781532113765 (lib.bdg.) | ISBN 9781532152641 (ebook)
Subjects: LCSH: Pyramids--Construction--Juvenile literature. | Egypt--Giza--Pyramids--Design-
        -Juvenile literature. | Pyramids of Giza (Egypt)--Juvenile literature. | Great Pyramid
        (Egypt)--Juvenile literature.
Classification: DDC 690.6--dc23
        LC record available at https://lccn.loc.gov/2017946940

CONTENTS

THE PYRAMIDS IN THEIR PRIME

I t is early morning in the workers' city at Giza, in ancient Egypt. It is the 2500s BCE. The sun rises over the Nile River, east of town. It lights up the eastern face of King Khufu's huge pyramid to the north. At the pyramid's peak, a shiny capstone reflects the sun.

Khufu has died. The pyramid is his tomb. But it's more than just a tomb. It is a symbol of the Egyptians' religious beliefs. It is also a marvel of ancient engineering.

An artist's rendering shows how Khufu's pyramid may have looked in ancient times.

FUNERALS IN ANCIENT EGYPT

The ancient Egyptians believed that death was not an end to life. It was a journey to eternal life. To prepare for a safe journey, a person had to honor the gods who ruled over Earth. When the person died, loved ones buried the body with tools, food, and drink. The person needed these items to journey through the world of the dead and reach eternal life in paradise.

Ordinary people were buried in the ground with some everyday objects and food. Important people were buried in tombs. The more important

WHY PYRAMIDS?

In ancient Egypt, a mound of earth was a symbol of new life. The people lived along the Nile River. Every year, the river rose and flooded the land nearby. When the water dropped again, it left behind rich soil. Plants grew there, starting on the highest mounds of earth. A pyramid stood for a mound of earth. It was a symbol of new life after a time of waiting.

The pyramids' incredible scale continues to impress visitors today, more than 4,500 years after their construction.

people were, the more elaborate their burials were. For example, elite Egyptians were sometimes mummified, or preserved. Their tombs contained many supplies. And the tombs themselves were often large and fancy.

BIG, FANCY TOMBS

The biggest, fanciest tombs are the pyramids. Some of Egypt's pharaohs, or kings, had pyramids built for themselves. When Khufu's son Khafre became king, he ordered his own pyramid built. Thousands of workers were needed to carry out this order. Khafre's pyramid rose slowly from the desert. It stands just southwest of Khufu's pyramid. Khufu's pyramid took about 20 years to build. Khafre's took about that long too. When Khafre died, his son Menkaure became pharaoh. He, too, had a pyramid built nearby.

The pyramids are massive. Khufu's, the largest, is 481 feet (147 m) tall. The pyramids are made of stone blocks weighing an average of 2.5 tons (2.3 metric tons) each. And the ancient Egyptians had

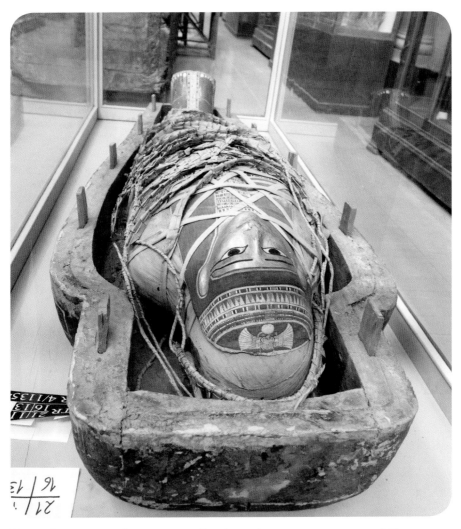

Egyptian mummies are on display at museums around the world, including this one in Cairo, Egypt.

only simple building tools. They made their own axes, chisels, and hammers from copper, wood, and stone. They didn't have pulleys or cranes. Those had not been invented yet.

WORKERS' GRAFFITI

The workers at Giza were highly organized. They were grouped into divisions. Each division had an inspiring name, such as Strength, Endurance, or Perfection. Several divisions made up a tribe. Five tribes made up a crew. Two crews made up a gang. Each gang had a name. The name always included the name of the king. For example, one gang was called the Friends of Khufu Gang. Another gang had a surprising name: the Drunks of Menkaure. Modern archeologists found these names in graffiti written on stone blocks inside the pyramids.

How did the ancient Egyptians build such amazing structures? They used early science and math to figure out how. They made the most of the knowledge, materials, and tools available to them to engineer one of the wonders of the ancient world.

STRAIGHT TO THE
SOURCE

Archaeologist Mark Lehner discussed the groups of workers who built the pyramids at Giza:

> There's some evidence to suggest that people were rotated in and out of the raw labor force. . . . If you were brought from a distance, you were brought by boat. Can you imagine floating down the Nile and—say you're working on Khafre's Pyramid—and you float . . . around this corner . . . and there's the Khufu Pyramid, the biggest thing on the planet. . . . And you see, for the first time in your life, not a few hundred, but thousands, probably, of workers and people as well as industries of all kinds. You're rotated into this experience . . . and then you're rotated out, and you go back . . . but you're not the same. You have seen . . . the Pyramids, the centralization, this organization. They must have been powerful socializing forces.

Source: "Who Built the Pyramids?" *PBS*. WGBH, February 4, 1997. Web. Accessed April 7, 2017.

What's the Big Idea?

Read this piece of Lehner's interview carefully. What does it tell you about how the pyramids were built? What does it say about ancient Egyptian society? Name two or three details that support these ideas.

PREPARING TO BUILD THE PYRAMIDS

Khufu wasn't the first pharaoh to build a pyramid. In fact, his father, Sneferu, built at least three of them. And before Sneferu, Djoser built Egypt's first pyramid.

During Sneferu's time, Egyptian pyramids changed from step pyramids to true pyramids. A step pyramid, such as Djoser's, has distinct layers. The biggest layer is on the bottom. On top of that goes a smaller layer. An even

The stepped pyramid of Djoser dates back to before the more famous true pyramids at Giza.

smaller layer comes next, and so on. The end product looks like a pyramid-shaped staircase. A true pyramid, such as Sneferu's third pyramid, has smooth sides.

Before Khufu could build his pyramid, he had to answer many questions. He chose a relative, Hemiunu, to help him. Khufu put Hemiunu in charge of designing and building all pyramids, temples, and palaces in Egypt.

CHOOSING A LOCATION

First, Hemiunu had to figure out where to

build Khufu's pyramid. It couldn't be just anywhere. He had to consider several key needs.

Ancient Egyptian religion said that Khufu's pyramid had to be west of the Nile River. The west was the land of Osiris, Egyptian god of the dead. Khufu's pyramid also had to be near Memphis. Memphis was the capital of ancient Egypt. Egypt's most powerful government officials lived there. Hemiunu needed their help to get enough materials and workers for this huge project.

Khufu's pyramid needed a lot of stone. It had to be near a large supply of limestone for the outer structure. It also needed a smaller supply of granite for the inner structure. Granite wasn't available near Memphis. It had to be shipped to the building site on boats. This meant the pyramid had to be fairly close to the river.

Hemiunu wanted to build Khufu the largest pyramid ever. And he wanted a site that was big enough for more pyramids. He hoped to create a vast burial ground for the royal family. He would need lots of space.

For thousands of years, the Nile River has made life in Egypt's desert possible.

Safety was important too. The building site had to be solid rock. It couldn't have any cracks. Cracks could make the rock foundation crumble under the pyramids' weight. And the site had to be above the Nile's yearly flood level.

The Giza Plateau was the only place that met
all these needs. It was on the west bank of the Nile
River. It was about 15 miles (24 km) north of Memphis
and 8 miles (13 km) west of the Nile. It was a massive
outcrop of solid limestone with an area of about

GIZA
PLATEAU

This diagram shows the Giza Plateau. After reading about it, what did you imagine it looked like? How has that idea changed? How does seeing this map help you better understand why Hemiunu chose this building site?

Menkaure's pyramid

Khafre's pyramid

Khufu's pyramid

Nile River

100 acres (40 ha). The plateau was well above the reach of the river during flood season. Another large outcrop of limestone lay nearby.

PLANNING, PLANNING, PLANNING

Once Hemiunu chose a location, he got busy planning. He figured the time needed for building. He'd watched the construction of Sneferu's third pyramid. It was 341 feet (104 m) tall with one burial chamber. It took 11 years. It rose about 30 feet (9 m) per year. Khufu's pyramid would be 481 feet (147 m) tall with three burial chambers. Hemiunu figured it would rise slower. It would take about 20 years.

Hemiunu also considered the king's age. Khufu was about 40 when he became king. Ancient people didn't live as long as modern people do. Khufu might die soon. So Hemiunu planned three burial chambers inside the pyramid. One was underground. It could be finished in five years. Another chamber was in the middle of the pyramid. It could be done in ten years. A third chamber

THE CUBIT

Ancient Egyptian builders measured things with their bodies. Their most important unit of measurement was the cubit. A cubit is the distance between the elbow and the tip of the middle finger. Because humans come in different sizes, a cubit is different from person to person. This was okay for small projects. But for big projects like pyramids, builders needed a unit that was always the same. So they used the royal cubit. A royal cubit is 20.6 inches (52.3 cm).

was high up in the pyramid. It could be finished in 20 years.

From Sneferu's experience, Hemiunu knew that he needed about 25,000 workers. About 5,000 people would cut stone blocks from the earth, move them to the pyramid, and set them in place. About 20,000 backup workers—carpenters, water carriers, overseers, cooks, doctors, and more—would support the builders. Hemiunu sent government officials to visit every corner of Egypt. They looked for healthy men willing to volunteer for their country's glory.

The largest pyramid, Khufu's, *rear right,* was placed so that it would not interfere with the construction of the later pyramids.

While the workers gathered, Hemiunu marked out the pyramid's base. The approach to the plateau was on the plateau's south end. Khufu's pyramid would be placed in the plateau's northeast corner. That way it wouldn't block the way of workers building later pyramids.

Ancient Egyptian religion said that the four sides of Khufu's pyramid must face exactly north, south, east, and west. Hemiunu had to figure out where north was. He may have measured the positions of a star on the horizon as it rose and set. Or he may have measured the positions of a stick's shadow as the sun rose and set. Then he drew a line exactly in the middle of these two positions. This line pointed precisely north. Now he could figure out south, east, and west.

The Giza Plateau was not perfectly flat. A giant pyramid couldn't sit safely on a slope. So Hemiunu had to level the building site. Leveling the entire area would be a long and tricky job. So instead, Hemiunu had workers simply level the outer edge of the site. Then they built a foundation platform with stone blocks. They carefully leveled the top of that platform. This created a flat base for the pyramid.

FURTHER EVIDENCE

Reread this chapter. Find its main point. List the key evidence you see to support that point. Then read the article at the website below. Find a quotation in the article that supports the chapter's main point. Does the quotation support a piece of evidence you found in the chapter or add a new one?

BUILDING THE GREAT PYRAMID
abdocorelibrary.com/engineering-pyramids-of-giza

BUILDING THE PYRAMIDS

Once Khufu's pyramid site was ready, building began. The construction project established a process that Khafre and Menkaure used later to build their own pyramids at Giza. The first step would be to find and prepare the stone.

STONECUTTING

Hemiunu needed more than two million blocks of stone for Khufu's pyramid. About 83 percent of the stone came from two limestone quarries

Over the years, engineers and illustrators have presented theories on how the pyramids were constructed, but many details are still unclear.

at Giza. One quarry sat at the base of Khufu's pyramid. Another quarry lay just south of the plateau. These quarries provided stone for the pyramid's core.

Giza limestone was rough, yellow, and full of fossils. It wasn't pretty enough for the pyramid's outer blocks, or facing. For the facing, Hemiunu chose fine white limestone. This came from a quarry at Tura. Tura was about 8 miles (13 km) south of Giza on the Nile's east bank.

Hemiunu wanted to build Khufu's main burial chamber with a flat ceiling. He needed strong stone for that. The ceiling would have to hold up hundreds of thousands of tons of stone. Limestone wasn't strong enough. But granite was. The granite came from a quarry at Aswan. Aswan was 500 miles (805 km) south, also on the Nile River.

The Aswan quarry was an important source of stone for several ancient Egyptian monuments.

Limestone is a soft stone. It splits along straight lines. It's easy to cut blocks from a limestone quarry. Workers hammered copper chisels and wedges into the stone with wooden mallets. They shaped and smoothed the blocks soon after cutting them. Limestone hardens after being in the open air for a while.

Granite is significantly harder than limestone. It was slow and difficult to cut with ancient Egyptian tools.

Khufu's main burial chamber needed more than 3,500 tons (3,175 metric tons) of granite by the twelfth year of building. So work at the Aswan quarry

CORBELED ARCHES

The Grand Gallery, a passage leading to Khufu's chamber, is a corbeled arch construction. To build a corbeled arch over an opening in a stone wall, the builder extends one end of a stone over each side of the opening and weights the other end of the stone. With each added row of stones, the end pieces extending over the opening get closer. Eventually they meet in the center.

INSIDE KHUFU'S
PYRAMID

This diagram shows the inside of Khufu's pyramid. After reading about the pyramid's construction, what did you imagine it looked like inside? How has that idea changed? How does seeing this diagram help you better understand the pyramid's design?

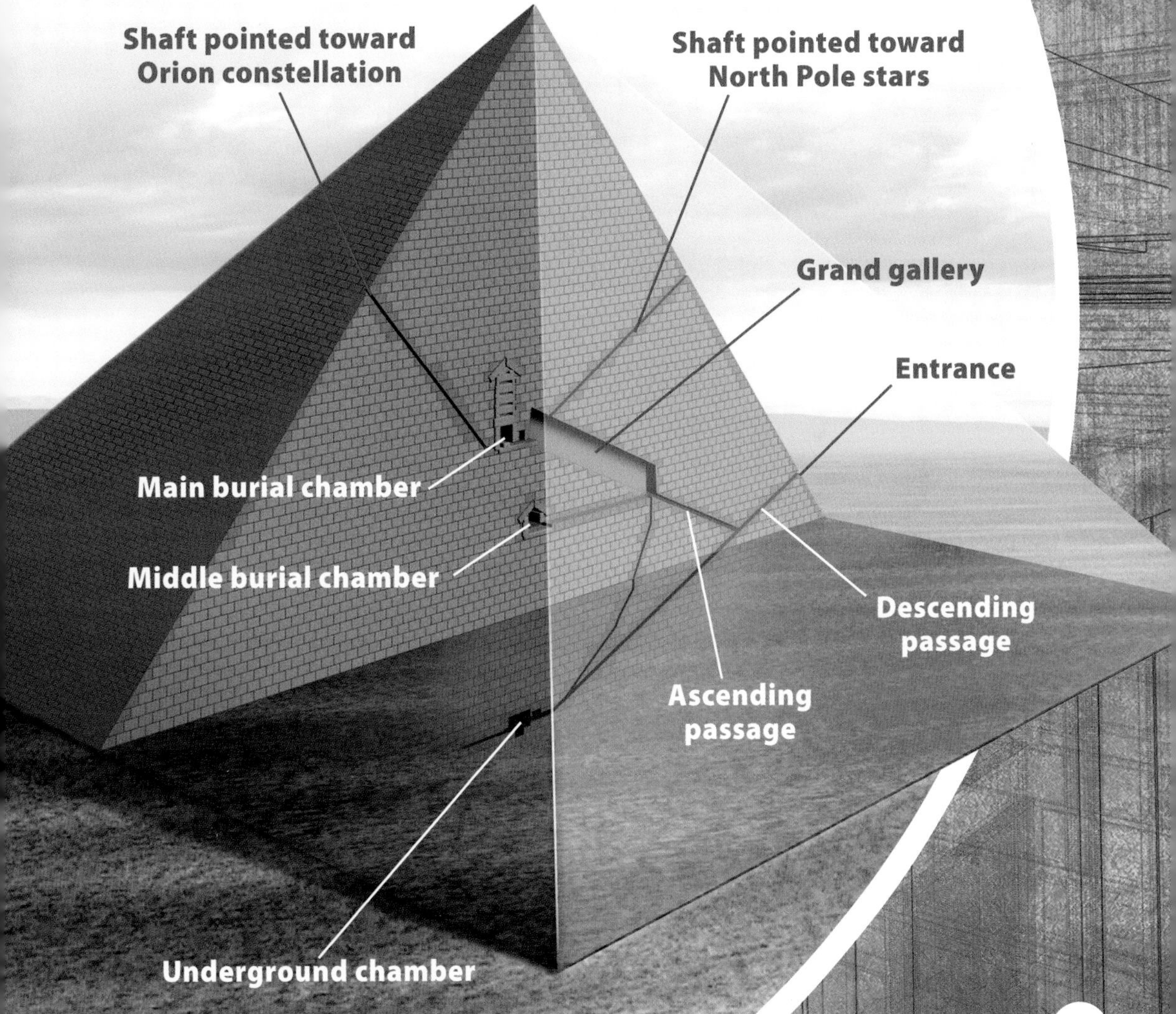

Shaft pointed toward Orion constellation

Shaft pointed toward North Pole stars

Grand gallery

Entrance

Main burial chamber

Middle burial chamber

Descending passage

Ascending passage

Underground chamber

started immediately. Workers dropped hard, heavy rocks onto the granite to chip away at it. They also cut the granite with copper saws or drills and a paste of hard quartz particles.

TRANSPORTING BLOCKS

The blocks varied in size and weight. They averaged 2.5 tons (2.3 metric tons) each. Workers moved blocks overland from the Tura and Aswan quarries to the Nile. They shipped the blocks to Giza on boats. Then they moved the blocks overland from the river to the pyramid. They moved the blocks from the Giza quarries overland too.

For overland transport, workers used cedar sleds on cedar rails. Workers coated the rails with mud. Water carriers ran to and from the river. They poured water on the rails to keep the mud wet. Wet mud made the rails slippery. More than 30 teams of up to 20 men each pulled the sleds along the rails by rope. They moved about 340 stone blocks per day.

LIFTING AND PLACING BLOCKS

Workers pulled and pushed the pyramid's base layer of stones into place. For higher layers, they had to lift the stones. They probably used ramps. Evidence of ramps still exists from pyramids older than Khufu's. But historians do not know what kind of ramps were used at Giza.

Several types of ramps are possible. All would have been made of mudbrick and rubble. A linear ramp would have stuck straight out from one face of the pyramid. A spiral ramp would have

PERSPECTIVES
LIFE IN THE WORKERS' CITY

Skilled workers, such as stonecutters, carpenters, and metalworkers, lived at Giza year-round. Laborers were farmworkers. They lived at Giza during the Nile's flood season, when farm fields were underwater. Even for the lowliest laborers, life was pretty good. They had snug shelter, security, and good medical care. They got plenty of meat and beer—more than they'd have had back home. They got a day of rest every ten days. The atmosphere mixed hard work with feasting and community pride.

hugged all four faces of the pyramid. An internal ramp would have been a spiral ramp hugging the insides of all four faces. An internal ramp may have been most likely, since there is no evidence for ramps on the plateau itself.

After lifting the blocks, workers laid them in place with wooden rockers. Then they filled the spaces between blocks with relatively small amounts of mortar. The mortar was made of a soft mineral called gypsum. Workers smashed it to a powder and mixed it with water to make a paste. The paste dried to a hard finish, like modern plaster. As the workers built each layer, they also built the pyramid's three inner chambers. Several passages and shafts linked the chambers to the outdoors.

To finish the pyramid, workers topped it with a pyramidion. This was a small pyramid made of diorite, granite, or fine limestone covered in gold, silver, or

A spiral ramp may have allowed workers and materials to ascend the pyramid during construction.

The pyramidion from the top of Khufu's pyramid is missing, but examples of other Egyptian pyramidions can be found in museums.

electrum, a mixture of gold and silver. Its underside was shaped to fit in a carved space so it wouldn't move. A religious ceremony and celebration followed the pyramid's completion.

STRAIGHT TO THE
SOURCE

The Greek historian Herodotus wrote a description of the Egyptian pyramids in about 450 BCE. Though his description of the construction was likely inaccurate, it brought the pyramids to wider attention:

> This pyramid was made after the manner of steps, . . . and when they had first made it thus, they raised the remaining stones with machines made of short pieces of timber, raising them first from the ground to the first stage of the steps, and when the stone got up to this it was placed upon another machine standing on the first stage, and so from this it was drawn to the second upon another machine; . . . the highest parts of it were finished first, and afterwards they proceeded to finish that which came next to them, and lastly they finished the parts of it near the ground and the lowest ranges.

> Source: *The History of Herodotus, Volume I.* New York: MacMillan, 1890. Web. Accessed April 4, 2017.

Back It Up

What evidence might Herodotus have relied upon when writing his account, and what kinds of different evidence might be available to modern archaeologists? Why might accounts like Herodotus's be useful, even if some details are proven incorrect?

CHAPTER
FOUR

THE PYRAMIDS TODAY

In the 100s BCE, Greek writers made a list of great monuments, now known as the Seven Wonders of the World. The Giza pyramids topped the list. They were the oldest of the wonders. Even 2,000 years ago, the pyramids were already 2,000 years old. They are the only ancient wonders still standing today. The United Nations Educational, Scientific, and Cultural Organization (UNESCO) named the Giza pyramids a World Heritage Site in 1979. This honor is designed to protect and preserve cultural and natural treasures.

The pyramids of Giza now sit near the modern city of Cairo, Egypt.

THE AGE OF THE PYRAMIDS

When reading about events that happened thousands of years ago, it can be hard to understand just how long ago that was. The pyramids were built around the 2500s BCE. In the 100s BCE, Greek writers made their list of the Seven Wonders of the World. That means that we are closer in time to those ancient Greeks than the Greeks were to the building of the Giza Pyramids.

People have admired the pyramids for a long time. But humans haven't been kind to the pyramids. They aren't as glorious as they once were. Over the centuries, thieves stole the valuable items buried with the pharaohs. They stripped off the white limestone facing. They toppled the pyramidions. Khufu's pyramid, without its pyramidion and facing, is now only 451.4 feet (138 m) tall. This is about 30 feet (9.1 m) shorter than its original height.

STILL STANDING

Despite four millennia of theft, earthquakes, and harsh desert weather, the pyramids still stand strong. That's because a pyramid is the steadiest shape possible for stone structures. It won't fall down on its own. And it's extremely hard to topple.

Because the pyramids are so stable, structural upkeep isn't a problem. But political turmoil is. In 2011, a revolution in Egypt ended the long presidency of Hosni Mubarak. The government has changed hands several times since. Security throughout Egypt has weakened. Several terrorist attacks have happened. Tourism is very important to Egypt, and Giza

PERSPECTIVES
THE PYRAMIDS' NEIGHBORHOOD

Back when the Giza pyramids were being built, they were way out in the desert. They were miles from ancient Egypt's capital city, Memphis. The pyramids' neighborhood has changed a lot in 4,500 years. The city of Giza developed there. Giza lies just southwest of Cairo, Egypt's modern capital. Together, Giza and Cairo form a huge metropolis. Photos taken from Giza make the pyramids look like they're still way out in the desert. But photos taken from the west or from the air show the huge city looming nearby.

Tourists from near and far flock to the pyramids to see one of history's greatest engineering achievements.

is Egypt's most important tourist site. Egypt is having a hard time attracting visitors to Giza. Visitors know that Egypt is struggling to keep both the tourists and the pyramids safe.

The government of Egypt has begun a series of scientific and historical projects to renew interest in its ancient artifacts, including the pyramids. For example, scientists working on a project called ScanPyramids are making very detailed scans of Sneferu's Bent Pyramid, Khufu's pyramid, and Khafre's pyramid. They hope these scans will reveal previously unknown chambers. They also hope the scans will help them finally understand exactly how the ancient Egyptians achieved these amazing feats of engineering.

EXPLORE ONLINE

Chapter Four describes the modern condition of the Giza pyramids and explains why they are still important. The website below offers a video showing what it would be like to visit the pyramids today. How is the information from the website the same as the information in Chapter Four? What new information did you learn from the website?

DESTINATION: EGYPT, PYRAMIDS

abdocorelibrary.com/engineering-pyramids-of-giza

FAST FACTS

- Ancient Egyptian pyramids are large, elaborate tombs for important people. They are also symbols of ancient Egyptian religious beliefs.

- In the 2500s BCE, the pharaohs Khufu, Khafre, and Menkaure reigned over Egypt. Each had a pyramid built. Khufu's pyramid was the first and largest. Khafre's was next. It's a bit smaller. Menkaure's pyramid was built last. It's much smaller. They're built in a line from northeast to southwest on the Giza Plateau.

- The Giza Plateau is a big limestone outcrop a few miles west of the Nile River. Workers built a canal to connect Giza with the Nile.

- Hemiunu, a relative of Khufu, was in charge of designing Khufu's pyramid. Hemiunu chose the Giza Plateau because it was on the west bank of the Nile, was near Memphis, and had plenty of space and solid limestone.

- Hemiunu employed about 25,000 workers. About 5,000 worked directly on Khufu's pyramid. About 20,000 supported the pyramid builders. The workers were paid volunteers. They worked hard but were also well fed and cared for.

- Khufu's pyramid contains three kinds of stone from four quarries.

- For distant transport of stone blocks, workers used boats. For overland transport, workers used cedar sleds on mud-coated cedar rails. Workers likely used ramps to raise blocks up the pyramid. A pyramidion topped each pyramid.

- The Giza pyramids are still standing today on the edge of a huge city. Thieves have stolen valuable artifacts, stripped the white limestone facing, and toppled the pyramidions. But the structures are still stable.

- The Giza pyramids are important to the Egyptian economy. Tourists spend a lot of money visiting them. Political turmoil in the area can cause security problems and reduce tourist numbers.

STOP AND THINK

Say What?

Studying ancient history can mean learning a lot of new vocabulary. Find five words in this book you'd never heard before. Use a dictionary to find out what they mean. Then write the meanings in your own words, and use each word in a new sentence.

Dig Deeper

After reading this book, what questions do you still have about the building of the Giza pyramids? With an adult's help, find a few reliable sources that can help you answer your questions. Write a paragraph about what you learned.

Why Do I Care?

The Giza pyramids were built 4,500 years ago. But that doesn't mean you can't find similarities between your life and the world of ancient Egypt. What building techniques and materials from the pyramids can still be seen in your world today?

You Are There

Chapters One and Three of this book discuss the experiences of workers who helped build Khufu's pyramid. Imagine you are a pyramid worker in ancient Egypt. Write 200 words about traveling to Giza, working on the pyramid, and living in the workers' city. What adventures do you have? What hardships do you endure? What do you enjoy?

GLOSSARY

archeologist
a scientist who studies human history through items left by ancient people

chisel
a tool with a long metal blade on one end and a handle on the other end

engineer
a person who is trained in developing and using nature's power and resources in ways that are useful to people

metropolis
a densely populated area

mummify
to keep a dead body from decaying by treating it with special chemicals and wrapping it in cloth strips

outcrop
a part of Earth's bedrock that sticks out of the ground

pharaoh
a ruler of ancient Egypt

plateau
a wide, flat area of high land

pyramidion
an ancient Egyptian pyramid's capstone

quarry
a place where people mine stone

wedge
a piece of wood or metal with a pointed edge used to split wood or rock

ONLINE RESOURCES

To learn more about the Pyramids of Giza, visit our free resource websites below.

Visit **abdocorelibrary.com** for free Common Core resources for teachers and students, including vetted activities, multimedia, and booklinks, for deeper subject comprehension.

Visit **abdobooklinks.com** for free additional online weblinks for further learning. These links are routinely monitored and updated to provide the most current information available.

LEARN MORE

Putnam, James. *Pyramid*. New York: DK, 2011.

Weitzman, David. *Pharaoh's Boat*. New York: Houghton Mifflin Harcourt, 2009.

INDEX

About the Author

Christine Zuchora-Walske studied literature, publishing, and communications at the University of Notre Dame and the University of Denver. She has been writing and editing children's books and articles for more than 20 years. Zuchora-Walske lives in Minneapolis, Minnesota, with her husband and two children.